ALWAYS LOVED

DEVOTIONAL SERIES

EXPERIENCING THE FATHER'S TENDERNESS
THROUGH EVERY SEASON OF LIFE

SPRING
A Time to Bloom

BRENT LOKKER

ALWAYS LOVED DEVOTIONAL SERIES
SPRING

.

Spring
A TIME TO BLOOM

Go slow. Explore with God. Enjoy the journey. See life as an adventure, not a test.

Seasons follow a cycle: winter, spring, summer, autumn...so that the Earth might enjoy all the things its Creator designed for it to enjoy. The same is true for our lives, changing seasons, not just one long monotonous journey. In the midst of all the landscape changes in this adventure we call life, our loving Father has one purpose above all: to enjoy an intimate friendship with Him along the way. He's a good, good Father!

Springtime ushers in fresh growth—new possibilities. Warmth returns and what once seemed dead springs forth to vibrant life. This is a season of Papa's refreshing and encouraging renewal. These are the times in your life when others will begin to see and be enriched by what God has been doing on the inside of you during the necessary winter seasons. This is your time to shine and let your voice be heard!

The one I love calls to me:
Arise, my dearest.
Hurry, my darling.
Come along with me!
I have come as you have asked
To draw you to my heart and lead you out.
For now is the time, my beautiful one.

The season has changed,
The bondage of your
Barren winter has ended,
And the season of hiding is over and gone.
The rains have soaked the earth

And left it bright with blossoming flowers.
The season for pruning the vines has arrived.
I hear the cooing of doves in our land,
Filling the air with songs
To awaken you and guide you forth.

Can you not discern
This new day of destiny
Breaking forth around you?
The early signs of my purposes and plans
Are bursting forth.
The budding vines of new life
Are now blooming everywhere.
The fragrance of flowers whispers,
"There is change in the air."
Arise, my love, my beautiful companion,
And run with me to the higher place.
For now is the time to arise
And come away with me.

SONG OF SONGS 2:10-13 (TPT)

You'll notice I use several different names for God in this devotional. I call Him Father, Papa, and even Daddy. I encourage you to know God, not as a distant, angry or indifferent Father, but as a close, kind and warm Father who loves to be with you. If being so tender and informal with

Him is new for you or even makes you uncomfortable, I encourage you to read my book *Always Loved: You are God's Treasure, Not His Project.*

Each week in this devotional you'll start by reading tender words from your heavenly Father, along with an encouragement from the Bible. I want you to re-read those same tender words every day of the week, allowing them to go deeper and deeper into your heart. Reading them out loud is especially helpful. I'll also ask you to respond to a question each day or have you engage with Papa's heart in one way or another. There's a half page of lines upon which to write your thoughts in response, but I've also left the bottom half of the page blank in case you would rather draw a picture or doodle in a way that speaks to the creativity within you.

The final day of each week I ask you to do something that's life-giving and to do it together with your heavenly Father. Why do I ask you to do this?

We're often so serious we forget to have fun along the way. Doing things you enjoy that bring more life to your heart is a significant part of God's plan for your life. So give yourself permission to do something life-giving (i.e. do a puzzle, make cookies, call an old friend, listen to music that inspires you, go on a hike and enjoy nature, etc.) but invite your Father to do it with you. When you're aware of Him enjoying life with you, whatever you're doing is enhanced.

Having said all that, since life is an adventure with Papa and not a test, I encourage you to use this devotional in whatever way helps you feel close to Him. After all, that is the goal!

Enjoy the journey into the depths of Papa's huge heart for you as His treasured child!

WEEK 1
You are Mine!

My precious child, you have no idea what you do to Me. You are My living treasure who has infinite worth to Me. You belong to Me. I chose you long before you knew who I was. You're still the one I choose and want to be with. Wild horses couldn't drag Me away from you! I want to be with you—not just for this moment— but for every moment throughout all eternity. You're stunning to Me and you're everything I always wanted. When I made you, you were My dream fulfilled! Your search for love and acceptance is over. Your longing for true intimacy with someone you can be real with is found with Me. I won't ask you to be anyone other than who you are. In our friendship, it's My choice to continually bless you not holding anything back from you. Come and enjoy Me just as I enjoy you.

READING FOR WEEK ONE

You must see what great love the Father has lavished on us by letting us be called God's children—which is what we are!

1 JOHN 3:1 (NJB)

The same way a loving father feels toward his children— that's but a sample of your tender feelings toward us, your beloved children, who live in awe of you!

PSALM 103:13 (TPT)

Your love is like a flooding river overflowing its banks with kindness. God, everyone sees your goodness, for your tender love is blended into everything you do.

PSALM 145:8-9 (TPT)

Each day this week, re-read Papa's kind words to you again, then go deeper by writing down or drawing your responses to the following questions:

DAY 1

What's the first response of your heart to these words from your Father?

DAY 2

How does it feel to be Papa's living treasure? Tell Him about it

_____

_____

_____

_____

_____

_____

_____

_____

DAY 3

When God says you have infinite worth to Him, they're not empty
words. The price for you was the sacrifice of Jesus on the cross. He says,
"You're worth everything to Me!" Ask Father to tell you in His own
words or show you in a picture just how important you are to Him.

DAY 4

How does it feel to know Papa desires to be with you and enjoys being with you? Ask Him to tell you why and write or draw what you sense from Him.

DAY 5

If you're not used to being real and transparent with God as a caring Father, perhaps it's because you weren't able to let the depths of your emotions out with your own parents growing up without being punished or shut down. Papa invites you to try again with Him right now and encounter His heart that wants genuine connection with you.

_____

_____

_____

_____

_____

_____

_____

_____

_____

DAY 6

Picture a river of God's kindness flowing right into your heart. His kindness is so extreme that you can't contain it all and so it overflows from you to those around you. One of the keys of God's kingdom is to know there's always more than enough. Write down or draw this encounter and what it's doing to you.

DAY 7

Do something that's life-giving today and do it together with
your heavenly Father. Write or draw what you did to remember
the fun you had with Him.

WEEK 2

You are My Masterpiece

When I crafted this beautiful earth with majestic mountains, raging seas, brilliant sunrises, vibrant flowers, fascinating animals of every kind and dreamy stars above, I called My creation *good*. It wasn't until I fashioned My crowning glory, sons and daughters made in My own image—including you—that I called all of My creation *very good!* You were never an afterthought to Me of how I could fill the Earth. I always had you in mind and I made the beauty of this earth for you to enjoy. You're the most astounding part of My creation.

When I formed you, I truly outdid Myself. I saved the best for last. So much so that the angels stood in disbelief and awe when they saw how I placed My very own Spirit within you. You are My masterpiece and the centerpiece of My creation. You are My poem and My living letter that speaks volumes to this world of Who I am. You are My song meant to be listened to as a beautiful melody played by a symphony of a lifetime of experiences, emotions, and special moments. Can you see the beauty of your life the way I can?

READING FOR WEEK TWO

Look at the splendor of your skies, your creative genius glowing in the heavens. When I gaze at your moon and your stars mounted like jewels in their settings, I know you are the Fascinating Artist who fashioned it all! But when I look up and see such wonder and workmanship above, I have to ask you this question: Compared to all this cosmic glory, why would you bother with puny, mortal man or be infatuated with Adam's sons? Yet what honor you have given to man, created only a little lower than Elohim (Creator God), crowned like kings and queens with glory and magnificence.

PSALM 8:3-5 (TPT)

We are engineered by his design; he molded and manufactured us in Christ. We are his workmanship, his poetry. We are fully fit to do good, equipped to give attractive evidence of his likeness in us in everything we do.

EPHESIANS 2:10 (TMT)

Each day this week, re-read Papa's kind words to you again, then go deeper by writing down or drawing your responses to the following questions:

20

DAY 1

What's the first response of your heart to these words from your Father?

DAY 2

Think back to one of the most beautiful places you've been and seen.
How does it feel to be God's crowning glory—His highest and best
creation—that surpasses the beauty of the Earth? Let that sink in and
journal or draw your impressions.

DAY 3

Imagine God painting you or meticulously fashioning you out of clay. He's taking His time to form you with stunning precision. Talk with Papa about any poor self-image you may have and allow Him to show you what's true.

DAY 4

Since you are God's poem that speaks of His goodness to the world,
listen to His heart and write a poem together with Him that captures
the beauty of your life.

DAY 5

Find a piece of classical music to listen to. As the intensity of the music increases and decreases, feel the tenderness of Papa's heart who's been faithfully by your side through the breathtaking symphony of your life, with all its ups and downs. Write or draw what you experience.

DAY 6

Ask Papa, "Show me the beauty of my life the way You see it." Sit with
Him for a while and write or draw what He shows you.

DAY 7

Do something that's life-giving today and do it together with your heavenly Father. Write or draw what you did to remember the fun you had with Him.

WEEK 3
You're Perfect For Me

My child, the enemy of your soul has lied to you to attempt to keep you imprisoned in shame. I tell you the truth: You're perfect for Me! My definition of perfection isn't to live without mistakes but to live according to your original identity! Be the real you that I created. Trying to imitate another—even one you admire greatly—will leave you feeling empty in the end. This is why comparing yourself to others is so damaging. I didn't make you to be like somebody else. Learn from Me who I've created you to be and the passions I've placed in your heart that bring you life and joy.

I'm not disinterested in your life, or simply a casual observer from a distance. I have intricately fashioned the details of your life to produce a beautiful fragrance that attracts others to the source of that beauty, just as a vibrant flower attracts a honeybee. The more you celebrate yourself in the same way I do, the brighter you will shine and the more others will be drawn to your light. As your confidence soars, you will change the atmosphere in a room full of people, not by what you say, but by who you are.

READING FOR WEEK THREE

By virtue of that one single offering, Jesus has achieved the eternal perfection of all who are sanctified.

HEBREWS 10:14 (NJB)

Every part of you is so beautiful, my darling. Perfect your beauty, without flaw within.

SONG OF SONGS 4:7 (TPT)

Each day this week, re-read Papa's kind words to you again, then go deeper by writing down or drawing your responses to the following questions:

DAY 1

What's the first response of your heart to these words from your Father?

DAY 2

In what ways recently have you expended great amounts of energy
attempting to live life mistake-free thinking this was God's plan for
you? Papa is giving you His permission to let yourself off the hook from
living in this way so you can enjoy life more without feeling shame.
Write or draw what you're feeling.

DAY 3

If you've been placing unrealistic expectations on yourself, you've almost certainly done that with others (probably without knowing it) leading to harshness and judgment in your heart. Ask for Papa's help to let others off the hook from living mistake-free and to simply love them in the same way He loves you. Write out that prayer.

DAY 4

Talk with Papa about His definition of perfection—being true to the real you He created. Ask Him to help you be more in touch with the genuine you that needs freedom to shine.

DAY 5

If your life has felt empty or without purpose, ask God to realign your heart to the passions He's placed within you. Then write down or draw what your heart feels.

DAY 6

Read out loud the Song of Songs passage that Jesus speaks
directly to you. Speak your own name in place of *my darling*.
"Every part of you is so beautiful, (your name).
Perfect your beauty, without flaw within."
Let this go deep. What is His truth doing to you?

DAY 7

Do something that's life-giving today and do it together with your heavenly Father. Write or draw what you did to remember the fun you had with Him.

WEEK 4

I Believe In You

My child, you measure up. You are enough. I didn't make you deficient or *less than* in any way. I approve of you! I have plans for you to be wildly successful—but trust Me to define what success looks like. Focus on enjoying the journey with Me! The sky is the limit for you, My precious one. Actually, in My kingdom, there are no limits!

You're doing so much better than you think you are. You've come so much further than you know. Keep going! My voice of assurance is the only one that matters. I believe in you even when you don't believe in yourself. I trust you. Really! Otherwise I wouldn't have empowered you with My Spirit to represent Me.

All of this is true because it's My decision to love you into health and to help you fulfill the destiny I have for you—and My decision is final! I am for you. What else really matters?

READING FOR WEEK FOUR

Now to Him who is able to do exceedingly abundantly above all that we ask or think, according to the power that works in us.

EPHESIANS 3:20 (NKJV)

And having chosen us, he called us to come to him; and when we came, he declared us "not guilty," filled us with Christ's goodness, gave us right standing with himself, and promised us his glory. What can we ever say to such wonderful things as these? If God is on our side, who can ever be against us?

ROMANS 8:30-31 (TLB)

Each day this week, re-read Papa's kind words to you again, then go deeper by writing down or drawing your responses to the following questions:

DAY 1

What's the first response of your heart to these words from your Father?

DAY 2

How does it feel to know you are already enough and that your heavenly Father is committed to your success? Talk with Him about it and feel His great heart for you.

_____

_____

_____

_____

_____

_____

_____

_____

_____

DAY 3

Ask God to show more of the reality of His kingdom where there are no limits and where all things are possible. Dream with Him about the good you could do with that kind of power. Write or draw what the two of you dream about together.

DAY 4

How does it feel to know Papa believes in you?

DAY 5

How does it feel to know Papa trusts you?

_____

_____

_____

_____

_____

_____

_____

_____

_____

DAY 6

How does it feel to know your heavenly Papa, Whose authoritative voice spoke the worlds and universes into existence, is for you at all times?

DAY 7

Do something that's life-giving today and do it together with your heavenly Father. Write or draw what you did to remember the fun you had with Him.

WEEK 5

You are Royalty

My Son/My daughter, because I am the Most High King, that make you part of My royal family. I invite you to rule and reign with Me, but only as you learn to do so with My heart. I'm a benevolent King and you are created to be like Me, releasing My kindness and justice, My love and mercy everywhere you go.

I've made you to be a warrior, bred for victory! My strong justice is rising up within you at this time in history. My justice is about making all wrong things right again. My justice isn't coming *against* you but it's *for* you and it's coming *against* the forces of evil that have been destroying My children. I'll teach you how to use My authority to make things right again. I'm leading you in a victory parade where love and justice prevail because you're co-laboring with Me as a benevolent king or queen in My kingdom. I'm your sharp sword that assures you of victory!

We'll change the world for better, not because of your strength but because of My choice to love and empower you to make it happen. While we're bringing about more good on the Earth, remember that what's of the utmost importance is the sheer joy of doing it together.

READING FOR WEEK FIVE

You are chosen people, a royal priesthood, a holy nation, people who belong to God. You were chosen to tell about the excellent qualities of God, who called you out of darkness into his marvelous light.

1 PETER 2:9 (NOG)

Who is like you, O victorious people? Yahweh is the shield that protects you and the sword that leads you to triumph. Your enemies will try to corrupt you, but you yourself will trample on their backs!

DEUTERONOMY 33:29 (NJB)

Each day this week, re-read Papa's kind words to you again, then go deeper by writing down or drawing your responses to the following questions:

DAY 1

What's the first response of your heart to these words from your Father?

DAY 2

Have you ever thought of yourself as royalty? What does it feel
like to be included in God's royal family as a king or queen?
Talk with Papa about it.

DAY 3

You've been invited by God to rule and reign with Him. Ask Papa for His loving heart to do so in a way that represents Him well. Write down this prayer or draw your impressions of how His heart will be conveyed through you towards others.

DAY 4

Ask Papa to show you what you look like from heaven's perspective as a warrior king or a warrior queen. Write down or draw what He shows you.

DAY 5

See yourself as a heavenly "Superhero of Justice" with the ability to make wrong things right again. Talk with Papa about the longings you have to make certain wrong things right again on the Earth and ask Him for His power and love to do it. Write or draw the transformation you can envision happening and the next steps God is giving you to take with Him.

DAY 6

Envision God as a powerful sword that goes before you to cut through darkness and usher in His light. With the Lord Himself as your sword, how can you lose? Look at the qualities of this sword that goes before you and write down or draw what you sense or see.

DAY 7

Do something that's life-giving today and do it together with your heavenly Father. Write or draw what you did to remember the fun you had with Him.

WEEK 6

You're My Child of Purpose and Destiny

Listen to My voice, My child. You're not stuck. You're not drowning. You're not going around the same old mountain again. You're My child of purpose and destiny! When I created you, I had a distinct purpose in mind for your life and I'm causing it to happen. It may not always look that way to you, but here is where you must trust Me. What I've prepared for you to do, I'll give you the ability and the intention to do.

I do not cause all things to happen, but I orchestrate them into a brilliant plan for good in your life. Therefore, I want you to thank Me for everything that's happened, because there is a much greater plan for your life than what you can see in the midst of your circumstances. Whatever you are going through, you are going *through*, not remaining in.

Along the way, no matter how big your perceived problems appear to you, I dwarf them with My extravagant goodness. No matter what the enemy attempts to do to sidetrack you, My jealous love for you trumps it with ease. No matter how badly you think you've blown it, My grace is enough and you have My permission to proceed with confidence because of Christ, who is in you. All things are working for you, never against you.

READING FOR WEEK SIX

So we are convinced that every detail of our lives is continually woven together to fit into God's perfect plan of bringing good into our lives, for we are his lovers who have been called to fulfill his designed purpose.

ROMANS 8:28 (TPT)

———————

It is God who, for his own generous purpose, gives you the intention and the powers to act.

PHILIPPIANS 2:13 (NJB)

———————

No matter what happens, always be thankful, for this is God's will for you who belong to Christ Jesus.

1 THESSALONIANS 5:18 (TLB)

Each day this week, re-read Papa's kind words to you again, then go deeper by writing down or drawing your responses to the following questions:

DAY 1

What's the first response of your heart to these words from your Father?

_____

_____

_____

_____

_____

_____

_____

_____

_____

_____

DAY 2

If you're feeling stuck in life, it's very okay to have a good cry with Papa about it. Then, ask Him to reassure you of His decision that you are His child of purpose and destiny. What's He conveying to your heart about this?

DAY 3

Take some time with your heavenly Dad to ask for His perspective on how He's brilliantly orchestrated circumstances to work in your favor and be sure to tell Him how thankful you are. You can write a prayer of thanksgiving for His kindness to you here.

DAY 4

Ask Papa to show you how your problems are being dwarfed by His
goodness in your life. Write down or draw what He shows you.

DAY 5

Ask Papa to show you how His jealous love for you easily trumps anything the enemy would try to do to sidetrack you from your purpose. Write down or draw what He shows you.

_____

_____

_____

_____

_____

_____

_____

_____

DAY 6

Ask Papa to show you how much His grace and mercy overshadow any ways in which you feel you may have disqualified yourself. Write down or draw what He shows you.

DAY 7

Do something that's life-giving today and do it together with your heavenly Father. Write or draw what you did to remember the fun you had with Him.

WEEK 7

I've Given You a Responsive Heart

I've put a new heart within you to be able to enjoy closeness and intimacy with Me. The heart I've placed within you is responsive and sensitive to My touch. No longer are you closed off to My voice or My expressions of love. I'm continuously activating your new heart by applying the paddles of a supernatural defibrillator and shocking your heart into ever-expansive life! I'm exhaling My warm breath over any chilled places of your heart to activate every bit of the love that's inside you.

When I look at your heart, I'm not looking at what you think I am. I'm not looking at your perceived failures. I'm looking at the huge *YES* in your heart for Me. And that's a heart I can use to change the world!

READING FOR WEEK SEVEN

I will sprinkle you with clean water, and you will be clean.
I will wash away all of your dirtiness, and you will be clean
and pure, free from the taint of idols. I will plant a new
heart and new spirit inside of you. I will take out your
stubborn, stony heart and give you a willing, tender heart of
flesh...you will be My people, and I will be your God.

EZEKIEL 36:25–28 (VOICE)

———

Belief begins in the heart and leads to a life that's right with
God; confession departs from our lips and brings eternal
salvation.

ROMANS 10:10 (VOICE)

Each day this week, re-read Papa's kind words to you
again, then go deeper by writing down or drawing
your responses to the following questions:

DAY 1

What's the first response of your heart to these words from your Father?

DAY 2

The miracle of what Jesus has done for us with his sacrifice on the cross is to exchange an old and broken heart for a new and whole heart. Be sure to let Papa know you want this exchange. It's why He sent His Son to us. Tell Him so and write out your desire as well as draw your new heart as seen from heaven's perspective.

DAY 3

What kind of load is lifted off of you when you know God has washed away all dirtiness and has made you clean? Write down or draw the before and after version of yourself.

_____

_____

_____

_____

_____

_____

_____

_____

DAY 4

Closeness and intimacy with your heavenly Father is a gift from Him which means it's something you receive. Accept His heart that He wants to be close to you. Ask Him just how much He wants this and capture what He speaks to you.

DAY 5

Because you now have a heart that is responsive and sensitive to Papa's touch, declare through a prayer or picture what you will now experience with Him.

_____

_____

_____

_____

_____

_____

_____

_____

_____

DAY 6

God is looking at the YES in your heart, not at your perceived failures. Ask Him to help you see the very same thing and watch how it changes your life.

DAY 7

Do something that's life-giving today and do it together with your heavenly Father. Write or draw what you did to remember the fun you had with Him.

WEEK 8
Heaven Is Invading Earth

I love you with a passion that surpasses everything you thought you knew about passion and I want us to rule My kingdom together. Of course, that means it has to be done according to My specs—with love, grace, honor, and mercy—but also with power, signs, and wonders. Together, we'll see the impossibilities of heaven invading this earth because My love and compassion and tenderness will be released in ever increasing measure.

The more I show you who I am and how I operate, the more you will become just like Me because what you can envision and experience you will become, from one level of My glory to another! Others will come to know the goodness of My heart through you the more you see and experience Who I truly am. As you agree with the magnitude of My heart that's within, you'll represent Me accurately to everyone you meet on the Earth. You'll love one person at a time and release freedom and healing wherever you go.

READING FOR WEEK EIGHT

This, then, is how you should pray: "Our Father in heaven, hallowed be your name, your kingdom come, your will be done, on Earth as it is in heaven."

MATTHEW 6:9–10 (NIV)

This resurrection life you received from God is not a timid, grave-tending life. It's adventurously expectant, greeting God with a childlike "What's next, Papa?" God's Spirit touches our spirits and confirms who we really are. We know who he is and we know who we are: Father and children."

ROMANS 8:15–16 (MSG)

Each day this week, re-read Papa's kind words to you again, then go deeper by writing down or drawing your responses to the following questions:

DAY 1

What's the first response of your heart to these words from your Father?

DAY 2

How does it feel to know Papa wants you to help Him rule His kingdom? Are you excited? A bit fearful or overwhelmed? Talk with Him honestly about it and write down your thoughts and any insights you get from Him.

DAY 3

Papa wants you to rule with Him in His kingdom using love, grace, honor and mercy as well as power, signs and wonders. Craft a prayer of what you need from Him to understand His kingdom so you can rule with His heart.

DAY 4

Ask to see Papa more—to experience His goodness and kindness—so you can be more like the One you love and release the sweetness of His fragrance to those around you. Compose a request or draw a picture of seeing Him more fully.

DAY 5

If our Father's kingdom in heaven comes to the Earth, what would
that look like for you? For your family? For your community? For your
nation? For the world? This is a dangerously wonderful prayer Jesus
taught us to pray. What's true in heaven that you'd like to see happen
on the Earth? Write it and declare it!

DAY 6

The daily life-adventure we have with our Father is supposed to be exciting. This life was never meant to be about marking time until we leave the Earth. Ask Him today to open your eyes and your heart to the adventure that awaits you. Write down or draw what's stirring in your heart as you pray this courageous prayer.

DAY 7

Do something that's life-giving today and do it together with
your heavenly Father. Write or draw what you did to remember
the fun you had with Him.

WEEK 9

You're Born to Change the World

I created you to know Me and to partner with Me to do great exploits! That means you and I are going to accomplish great things that cause others to scratch their heads and wonder how it's even possible. I made you to live in a supernatural, extraordinary way because I made you to change the world. Being made in My image, you're great beyond measure. You aren't arrogant or prideful to believe this, you are simply agreeing with the truth of who I say you are. At the moment of your spiritual birth when you became aware of Jesus as your Savior, I infused you with the same resurrection power that raised Him from the dead!

As you seek My counsel, I will give you My supernatural wisdom to uncover brilliant solutions to issues that currently plague the world. You aren't responsible to solve all the problems of the world, but you will play a significant role in making wrong things right again. Changing the world will require great courage. I'm strengthening you with My lion's courage for you to know you're alive to make Earth look more and more like heaven.

READING FOR WEEK NINE

The people who know their God shall be strong,
and carry out great exploits.

DANIEL 11:32 (NKJV)

I want you to know about the great and mighty power that
God has for us followers. It is the same wonderful power he
used when he raised Christ from death and let him sit at his
right side in heaven.

EPHESIANS 1:19-20 (CEV)

If you don't have all the wisdom needed for this journey, then all
you have to do is ask God for it; and God will grant all that you
need. He gives lavishly and never scolds you for asking.

JAMES 1:5 (VOICE)

Each day this week, re-read Papa's kind words to you
again, then go deeper by writing down or drawing
your responses to the following questions:

DAY 1

What's the first response of your heart to these words from your Father?

DAY 2

To be a part of great exploits—bold and daring feats—with God, you
must first agree you are positioned by God to do this. Talk with Papa
and ask Him if this is truly His plan for you and He to change the
world together for good. What are you sensing from Him? And are you
ready to agree with Him?

DAY 3

Do you struggle with thinking you are arrogant or prideful if you believe you are great beyond measure because Papa made you that way? Talk with Him about it and ask for His help to move past false humility designed by the enemy to shut you down.

DAY 4

True humility is knowing that your life is a display of God's character so that others are drawn to Him. Being your true self is a gift to Him! Offer your life, the way He designed it to be, as a gift to Papa. Write it out or draw a picture to express this gift to Him.

DAY 5

Ask for Papa's help to be excited about the change you get to
bring about on the Earth, but not to feel weighed down or
stressed out about the big picture.

DAY 6

Where has God given you a desire to set wrong things right again? It may be within your family, within your school or workplace, within your community, or even larger issues that plague the world. Ask Him for His supernatural wisdom and write down the impressions you get. Ask Him for the next step you should take.

DAY 7

Do something that's life-giving today and do it together with your heavenly Father. Write or draw what you did to remember the fun you had with Him.

_____

_____

_____

_____

_____

_____

_____

_____

WEEK 10

You Have My Authority

All authority comes from Me. I gave My son Jesus full authority in heaven and on Earth and He's shared His authority with you who follow Him. To use My authority accurately, listen and agree with the words of My son Jesus who says to you:

You're a purebred from heaven, just like Me. You're made of what I'm made of and what's Mine is yours. What I freely received from My Father in heaven, I've freely given to you. Let's all use the authority Dad's given us to go and rock the world with His love, kindness and power. I've shown you how to do this through the example of My life on the Earth, and now I'll go with you to the ends of the Earth that God so loves because I'm your true Brother and I've got your back. We're family and that makes releasing our Father's love, healing and freedom a family business! What I accomplished on the Earth was just the start of what I'm accomplishing through all of My followers throughout the world and across the ages, including you. That makes you a part of something enormously important that's so much bigger than yourself.

READING FOR WEEK TEN

Jesus...gave his charge: "God authorized and commanded me to commission you: Go out and train everyone you meet, far and near, in this way of life, marking them by baptism in the threefold name: Father, Son, and Holy Spirit. Then instruct them in the practice of all I have commanded you. I'll be with you as you do this, day after day after day, right up to the end of the age."

MATTHEW 28:18-20 (MSG)

Go and announce to them that the Kingdom of Heaven is near. Heal the sick, raise the dead, cure those with leprosy, and cast out demons. Give as freely as you have received!

MATTHEW 10:7-8 (NLT)

For sure, I tell you, whoever puts his trust in Me can do the things I am doing. He will do even greater things than these because I am going to the Father.

JOHN 14:12 (NLV)

Each day this week, re-read Papa's kind words to you again, then go deeper by writing down or drawing your responses to the following questions:

DAY 1

What's the first response of your heart to these words from your Father?

DAY 2

The only way to gain genuine authority is to receive it from someone who has greater authority than yourself. Ask Papa to tell you what authority He's given you through Jesus and to show you in such a way that you know you've been fully empowered to carry out His wishes.

DAY 3

Jesus says to you, "What's mine is yours." Write down or draw all that belongs to Jesus to gain a fuller understanding of the immensity of this statement. (Reading 1 Corinthians 3:21- 23 will help you grasp the totality of what you've been given.)

DAY 4

Everything that's been given to you by Jesus (love, acceptance, forgiveness, mercy, healing, freedom, etc.) is to be freely given to others to make their lives better. Ask Him to show you how you can be more intentional about giving away to others the immense gifts you've been showered with. Write down or draw your impressions.

DAY 5

How does it make you feel to know that Jesus is continuing His ministry on the Earth through you because this is a family business? Since you are never alone, what will that give you the courage to do?

DAY 6

Jesus said you would do even greater things than He did when He was on the Earth. Everything He did was by the power of the Holy Spirit. Craft a prayer asking Holy Spirit to embolden you and empower you to carry out your part of releasing heaven's reality on the Earth.

DAY 7

Do something that's life-giving today and do it together with your heavenly Father. Write or draw what you did to remember the fun you had with Him.

WEEK 11

You're My Ambassador

I've empowered you as My ambassador to represent Me on this Earth. As My ambassador, I give you all of the rights and privileges of your true place of origin—My heavenly home. My goodness has made a home in you. My joy resides in you. My peace dwells in you. My loving-kindness is embodied in you. My kingdom and My sweet presence are inside of you! What you've freely received from Me, go give away to others. I've given you My authority to represent My heart to the people of this world who are My children even if they don't know it yet. I want you to let them know I am for them and not against them—how I love them as My very own. Tell them they are included. Tell them they are wanted. Tell them they are invited to join My everlasting family. I know you'll represent Me well because I've deposited a measure of My own uplifting character and Spirit inside of you.

By experiencing My deep love for you and enjoying My extravagant goodness, your life will bear unimaginable fruit for My kingdom. A life that's at rest in My love will inevitably pour out that same love to others. As you learn to enjoy a deep, loving relationship with Me, expect spontaneous, healthy growth. In the same way you are transformed by My love, you'll be a part of transforming others with that same love. Nothing can stop the power of My love from transforming My children and the world you live in.

READING FOR WEEK ELEVEN

Watch what God does, and then you do it. ... Mostly what God does is love you.

EPHESIANS 5:1 (MSG)

And all of this is a gift from God, who brought us back to himself through Christ. And God has given us this task of reconciling people to him. For God was in Christ, reconciling the world to himself, no longer counting people's sins against them. And he gave us this wonderful message of reconciliation. So we are Christ's ambassadors; God is making his appeal through us. We speak for Christ when we plead, "Come back to God!"

2 CORINTHIANS 5:18-20 (NLT)

Each day this week, re-read Papa's kind words to you again, then go deeper by writing down or drawing your responses to the following questions:

DAY 1

What's the first response of your heart to these words from your Father?

DAY 2

How does it feel to be an ambassador of heaven, knowing you have God's authority to represent Him on this earth? Talk with Him about it and ask for help if you need to know how to represent His heart accurately.

DAY 3

Do you believe Papa's goodness lives in you? If so, ask Him to show you why. If not, ask Him to show you who you are and what you carry.

DAY 4

You can only give away what you have. Ask God to show you just how much of His joy, peace, loving-kindness and sweetness you've been entrusted with and to give you an intentionality to release it today wherever you go. At the end of today, write down an encounter that happened.

DAY 5

You have been given the message of reconciliation. God made things right through the sacrifice of Jesus. How will this change your conversation with those you want to reach with the love of God?

_____

_____

_____

_____

_____

_____

_____

_____

_____

DAY 6

Love, not criticism, is the healthy environment we all need to grow. Ask Papa to infuse you with a supernatural dose of love, specifically so you can love (not criticize) others in their pain, helping them to grow into their true selves. At the end of the day, write down how you responded with love to someone in pain today.

DAY 7

Do something that's life-giving today and do it together with your heavenly Father. Write or draw what you did to remember the fun you had with Him.

WEEK 12

Love Others— Don't Judge Them

It's not your job to fix people nor is it your job to judge them. It's your job to love others just as I've loved you. How is it that you came to know Me? Was it because you were so clever in figuring it out? Or was it because I first showed you My compassionate love, tender kindness, and extravagant mercy, and then you responded to Me? You had no ability to find Me otherwise. I sovereignly touched your heart in a way you couldn't reason away. I broke through your walls of pain, defenses, and indifference. I made Myself irresistible, freely offering you the acceptance and forgiveness you so desperately needed. I'm asking you to do the same for everyone you encounter. If you choose instead to judge someone instead of extending My love and mercy, you'll lose the ability to reach them and I'll use someone else to do so instead.

People who are hurt and confused and making poor choices don't need to clean themselves up and make good choices in order for Me to find them. I'll reach them through you right where they're at and once I've restored their hope again, their heart will begin to trust and accept the good plan I have for their lives. Remember that you, too, became more healed and free one step at a time. Don't overlook My kindness to you and don't expect it to be different for someone else. Make it your choice to love and not to hate. You're to be My bright beacon of hope to those who are desperate and lonely.

READING FOR WEEK TWELVE

The wonder of love is not that we loved God, but that He first loved us enough to send His Son to remove the barrier that our sins had erected between us and him.

1 JOHN 4:10 (BNT)

You, therefore, have no excuse, you who pass judgment on someone else, for at whatever point you judge the other, you are condemning yourself, because you who pass judgment do the same things.

ROMANS 2:1 (NIV)

If any one of you is without sin, let him be the first to throw a stone at her.

JOHN 8:7 (NIV)

Mercy triumphs over judgment.

JAMES 2:13 (NIV)

Each day this week, re-read Papa's kind words to you again, then go deeper by writing down or drawing your responses to the following questions:

DAY 1

What's the first response of your heart to these words from your Father?

DAY 2

Take some time to remember what your life was like and the direction it was headed before God's love captured your heart. This would be a wonderful time to express a boatload of gratitude to Him for choosing to love you and completely forgive you.

DAY 3

Ask Papa to show you the ways in which you've judged others instead of choosing to love them. When He shows you areas of your heart that need adjusting, it's always with mercy and kindness and always to help you into a more mature place of love.

DAY 4

Sometimes we're afraid of being associated with someone who's making poor life choices. Jesus wasn't! He really didn't care what others thought about such things. Talk with Papa about this and write down or draw what He shows you.

DAY 5

Since it's not your job to clean people up for God to somehow make them more acceptable and it's only your job to love and accept them, how will that change some of the relationships you currently have?

DAY 6

Ask Papa what it looks like for you to be a bright beacon of hope to those who are desperate and lonely. Do something with Papa today to reach out to one of these hurting, lonely ones.

DAY 7

Do something that's life-giving today and do it together with
your heavenly Father. Write or draw what you did to remember
the fun you had with Him.

_____

_____

_____

_____

_____

_____

_____

_____

WEEK 13
Be My Voice

The truth of My affectionate heart for My children will once again be heard in bars, in the clubs, out on the street corners and in every place where a hungry heart is longing for My love. But this time those who share about Me will reflect My heart accurately. It won't be shouts of fear or judgment, but expressions of mercy and tender love. Even though people misunderstood My heart and caused great damage in previous times, choose to be My voice today.

You'll see signs of heaven's reality breaking into Earth's realm unlike anything you've ever seen. My transforming love will heal wounded hearts like never before. Don't underestimate the power of My love and the power of your voice that calls out to the lost, the hurting, and the broken. Declare life!

You're making a bigger difference in this world than you know. Keep going! Every single time you share a portion of My love in your heart with another, you're making a tangible difference. From heaven's perspective, every smile, kind word, act of kindness or display of mercy towards another not only impacts that person's life, but also causes a ripple effect that makes its way around the world. Go and search for My sons and daughters and bring them back home to My heart!

READING FOR
WEEK THIRTEEN

Mimic God; you are His offspring. This is how, let love be your life; equal to the love of Christ in the way He abandoned Himself to us. His love is contagious, not reluctant but extravagant. Sacrificial love pleases God like the sweet aroma of worship.

EPHESIANS 5:1–2 (TMT)

_____

The only things that register on God's scoreboard are taking God at his word and loving people....You were picked to be free. But it's not a "license to kill" (or whatever else the Old You fancies doing)— no, it's a freedom to work for other people's benefit 'cos you love them.

GALATIANS 5:6, 13 (WOTS)

Each day this week, re-read Papa's kind words to you again, then go deeper by writing down or drawing your responses to the following questions:

DAY 1

What's the first response of your heart to these words from your Father?

_____

_____

_____

_____

_____

_____

_____

_____

DAY 2

Make a choice today with Papa to be a clear and resounding voice of His love to those who are longing to know His Father's blessing and approval! Declare it in writing or draw what this looks like.

DAY 3

The healing of broken and disillusioned hearts is God's agenda for this hour. Ask Him to show you the hearts of those you are close to who need His healing touch upon their hearts. Craft a prayer declaring that His love will draw in the ones that you love.

_____

_____

_____

_____

_____

_____

_____

_____

_____

_____

_____

_____

DAY 4

You have the authority to declare life where the enemy has tried to steal it. Use your voice! Who is Papa placing on your heart that you need to declare life over?

_____

_____

_____

_____

_____

_____

_____

_____

DAY 5

Make it a point today to be aware of the power of a smile, a kind word, a small gesture of mercy and how it makes an eternal difference. Write down what happened as a remembrance. One day in heaven, Jesus will tell you the full impact of the ripple effect!

DAY 6

Go on a search today with Papa to look for a son or daughter who is longing to come back home. Remember, you're the one who leads them to the reality and love of Jesus and it's the Lord who draws them into Himself. One son or daughter is worth everything to Papa! Record what happens and keep your eyes open day after day!

DAY 7

Do something that's life-giving today and do it together with your heavenly Father. Write or draw what you did to remember the fun you had with Him.

Blessing

FINAL THOUGHTS

Receive this prayer of the Father's blessing over you:

*Father, out of Your honorable and glorious riches, strengthen Your
people. Fill their souls with the power of Your Spirit so that through
faith the Anointed One will reside in their hearts. May love be the
rich soil where their lives take root. May it be the bedrock where their
lives are founded so that together with all of Your people they will have
the power to understand that the love of the Anointed is infinitely
long, wide, high, and deep, surpassing everything anyone previously
experienced. God, may Your fullness flood through their entire beings.*

*Now to the God who can do so many awe-inspiring things,
immeasurable things, things greater than we ever could ask or imagine
through the power at work in us, to Him be all glory in the church and
in Jesus the Anointed from this generation to the next, forever and ever.
Amen.*

EPHESIANS 3:14-21 (VOICE)

Enjoy the never-ending journey of life with your heavenly Father who
has a bright and energizing future for you!

With Love,

Brent

LOOK FOR ALL FOUR BOOKS IN THE
ALWAYS LOVED DEVOTIONAL SERIES

TAKE A JOURNEY INTO THE DEPTHS OF
THE FATHER'S HEART

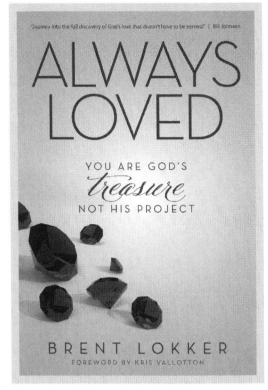

EXPERIENCE GOD'S AFFECTION FOR YOU
AS HIS SON OR DAUGHTER

Brent's powerful yet tender stories woven into truths from the Scriptures will draw you into a journey of intimacy with your heavenly Father. The more you receive His extravagant love, the more it pours forth from you as the world changer you are destined to be.

> "Chapter by chapter, you will journey into the full discovery of God's love that doesn't have to be earned. You will be encouraged by realizing who you are in the Father's eyes, which then makes it normal to truly love the broken and carry out great exploits." | **Bill Johnson**, Author of *Hosting the Presence* and *When Heaven Invades Earth*

Available at www.BrentLokkerMinistries.com.